# THE

# M⊙nsteR

# GUIDE TO
# EXCELLENT EXCUSES

WRITTEN BY
FRAN PICKERING

CREATED & ILLUSTRATED BY:
JOHN PICKERING

Kingfisher

KINGFISHER
An imprint of Larousse plc
24-30 Great Titchfield Street
London WIP 7AD

Copyright © Larousse plc 1996
Text copyright © Fran Pickering 1996
Illustrations copyright © John Pickering 1996

First published by Larousse plc 1996

10 9 8 7 6 5 4 3 2 1

A CIP catalogue record for this book is available from the British Library

ISBN 0 7534 0028 6

Printed in the United Kingdom

## Welcome to this
## MONSTER GUIDE BOOK

## This is NOT a Monster-sized Book about Guides...
## ...it is, in fact, A Book About
## BEING MONSTROUS

Sometimes **Monstrous** things just happen - for example, you may be out walking on a nice, sunny day, barefoot and carefree across a lovely green meadow, when suddenly, SPLOT! You step into a wet, smelly cow pat! What a **Monstrous** thing to happen.

Sometimes when we are supposed to be good and polite a **Monstrous** idea will suddenly pop into our minds – for example: you may be out with your Mum visiting some boring relative who never stops talking, when it occurs to you that it would be much more interesting to examine the contents of your nose! Suddenly your Mum shrieks: 'Stop that at once! That's a **Monstrous** thing to do in public!'

Which of course it is! That being the whole point of doing it in the first place!

Mostly though, adults do not appreciate this point of view!

This is because, generally, they do not have such **Monstrous** imaginations as children and do not find it easy to see things from the **Monster viewpoint**!

Obviously this can cause all kinds of misunderstandings and you may have often wished for the benefit of some expert advice. Well, here it is at last, in easy-to-read gobbits of **Smelly Secrets**, **Horrible Hints** and all kinds of **Monstrous Mayhem** neatly packed into your own, your very own:

...MONSTER GUIDE!

Aaargh! Aaargh! They're at you again! Don't panic. Help is at hand! If they think you're a little horror, and you think they're unreasonable monsters, then what you need are some

**EXCELLENT EXCUSES**

for:

\* *not* **doing your homework**

\* *not* **doing your chores**

\* *not* **being where you're supposed to be -**

**or having to be where you don't want to be!**

So, get your little mitts turning over the pages and discover the A to Z of excellent excuses for little monsters everywhere!

## ACTING YOUR AGE
(As in: 'Why don't you act your age?')

This is a question parents and teachers often seem impelled to ask. Why, we don't know! It seems stupid - how can you act an age you already are? If you find yourself short of monstrous inventiveness here are a few excellent replies guaranteed to blow some brain cells:

**Dramatic:** Fall to your knees, head in hands, sobbing: *'I've been practising acting my age since I was born. How can you criticise a lifetime's work? If you undermine my confidence like this there's nothing left for me.'* Tears are a vital element of this response, so keep a raw onion handy in your pocket and take a good sniff of this while your face is buried in your hands. That should bring tears to your eyes. Of course, if you could somehow contrive to have a hosepipe fixed to the kitchen tap and running up the back of your shirt, then you can produce floods of tears, on tap, as it were...

**Scientific:** Assume a serious look, take a deep breath, and give a dry cough to ensure your audience's rapt attention. You need to make your talk as boring as possible and show evidence of serious thought. Quoting a few chapters of the **Origin of the Species** should help.

ALTHOUGH EINSTEIN'S THEORY OF RELATIVITY SHOWS THAT THE MOVEMENT OF A BODY CURVES SPACE IT IS STILL RELATIVELY IMPOSSIBLE FOR A PERSON TO BE ANY AGE OTHER THAN THEY ARE IN THE CURRENT TIME CONTINUUM AND...

**Wacky:** Run round the room, screaming: *'Help! Help! There's a green worm inside my head!'* Or, get a large bowl of cold rice pudding and simply sit in it.

**Paranormal:** Shriek loudly and spin round and round, crying: *'Oh dear! Have you found me out? Since inhabiting the body of this strange creature I've been trying to act in every way that would seem normal. I must now resume my natural shape and behaviour!'* Of course, if you want to enjoy your tea or get your pocket money at the end of the week, the answer least likely to cause trouble is: *'I'm sorry, I won't do that again.'*

### Why are you still awake?

This question often comes with the addition – *you should be asleep* – as if you were breaking some universal law. If you're awake because you're worried about something, then tell an adult what you are worried about and get it sorted out. However, sometimes you don't *know* why you're still awake. That's when a Little Monster would liven up events with an excellent excuse such as this one: *Pretend to be sleepwalking. Sit up slowly and, with eyes open and arms outstretched, walk past the questioner and head for the fridge. Help yourself to some food, go and turn the TV on and sit there eating. Ignore all that is said to you. Do all this in a slow, dream-like state, keeping your eyes as wide as possible.*

A WORD OF **ADVICE** – DON'T LOOK OUT OF THE WINDOW AT NIGHT OR THEY'LL THINK IT'S HALLOWE'EN!

WHY AREN'T YOU PAYING **ATTENTION?**

This is one of those irritating questions that teachers and parents have a knack of asking whenever you are: dropping off to sleep – figuring out how to beat your last score in your favourite computer game – or wondering what exactly that slimy, sticky thing in your pocket is!

A quick, effective answer to this in the classroom situation is to let your eyelids droop, flop face forwards onto your desk, give a little sigh and start snoring gently but audibly! When they start shaking you, start muttering: *'No, no, I can't fill another box!'* When questioned as to the meaning of this, sit up sleepily and explain that your parents are suffering from a cash flow problem and that you have to work nights packing in a chocolate factory to buy your own clothes. With any luck the teacher will let you go and lie down while the class discuss how much they can raise towards your keep!

Or you could try:

**Paranormal:** *'Oh, sorry, I was being contacted by my spirit guide, who just happens to be Plato, and he agreed with everything you said, 'cos it was all Greek to him!'*

**Psychological:** *'I'm sorry, I was still considering your previous comments, which I found truly fascinating and kind of spun me off on a mental tangent. Perhaps you could just reiterate your last point for me.'*

## A is also for **Alien Abduction**

In a tricky classroom situation where you don't know the answer to the question the teacher has just asked, but are picked on to demonstrate this to the whole room, it is often really useful to be on good terms with any passing aliens. If you don't know any friendly aliens, you'll just have to fake it:

*Rise from your chair and go suddenly rigid. With eyes wide and staring, cry in a hoarse voice* 'Aaargh! They're coming for me!' *Then collapse in slow motion over your desk! When the teacher starts to shake you, open your eyes slowly and say,* 'Who are you? Am I back on Earth?' *Then tell them that the last thing you remember was a bright light filling the classroom and an alien being saying:* 'Don't be afraid, all we want is to learn everything that you know!' *Tell them how you were beamed up in astral form to the hovering craft where everything you had learnt over the past six months was sucked out. As proof of this, ask the teacher to test you on some elementary facts – you can then truly astound the class with a convincing display of total ignorance.*

## MATHS TEST

For any sum with numbers that exceed the combined digits of your fingers and toes put:

a) $\pi^2$ *or* b) 1 zillion

BUT, if you really want to impress your teacher with your ability to work out a tough problem, try simply adding all the numbers together! For example 21 February 1994 turned into numbers = 21/2/1994.

Add the numbers together like this:

$$21 + 2 = 23 \qquad 2 + 3 = 5$$
$$1 + 9 = 10 \qquad 1 + 0 = 1$$
$$9 + 4 = 13 \qquad 1 + 3 = 4$$

Now add the three answers together, like this:

$$5 + 1 + 4 = 10$$
$$1 + 0 = 1.$$

The answer is 1, as you have no more numbers!

## HISTORY TEST

For questions about dates try either 1066 or just put down your own birthday in Roman Numerals! There are lots of people in history, but as most of them are Julius Caesar, Napoleon, Ghengis Khan, Richard the Lionheart, Boadicea or Florence Nightingale, put down one of these for any character question and you won't be far wrong!

# GEOGRAPHY TEST

For any question about climate always put: **rain** as it is always raining somewhere most of the time! Questions about places can be a bit tricky. There are a lot of places in the world, but usually your teacher only wants ones you've never heard of. So if you haven't heard of any of the following put one of those: **Barrow-in-Furness, Drogheda, Jyvaskyla, Kwanchow, Xingu, Zumbo!**

For any difficult general questions always put: **London**, **New York**, **Volcano**, **NATO** or **The Sahara Desert**! If you get a really obscure question just put, **Brussels**.

## SCIENCE TEST

Science is a vast subject, but if you categorise, you'll find it much easier to deal with! Here are answers for all those difficult questions:

<u>**Chemistry:**</u> bunson burner, $H_2O$, iron filings, carbon dioxide *or* test tube.

<u>**Physics:**</u> atoms, electromagnet, relativity *or* Albert Einstein!

<u>**Biology:**</u> DNA, frogspawn, enzyme, *or* Venus Fly Trap!

<u>**Astronomy:**</u> Mars, The Milky Way, Halley's Comet, Neil Armstrong *or* The Sun!

Of course, the best way to avoid thinking about a hard question in any test is to just write next to it: see attached sheet! Then attach a blank piece of paper which will accurately describe your state of mind!

IF YOU READ THE DICTIONARY EVERY NIGHT YOU'LL HAVE AN ANSWER FOR EVERYTHING!

**A** is also for **Analogy**

This is a thing you should know for English composition and writing an' stuff! If in a test or lesson you get asked to give an analogy, (just quickly copy this page now and you'll have it ready!), trace the illustration below onto a piece of paper, and remember...

**Analogy** is a bug that can only be seen with a microscope. Usually in books, when a person sneezes or is ill, they are said to have analogy, and writers like to put analogy in when they can't think of anything else to say!

A picture is worth a thousand words so your teacher is going to be really impressed with this picture of analogy!

# BRAINS

(As in: 'Haven't you got any?')

Another stupid question often asked by people who should know better! The safe response is to keep quiet and look ashamed or sorry. Can we trust a Monster to do the right thing? No...

If you don't have anyone else's brains to offer the genius who is asking you the question, you could try the logical response. Ignore the question entirely and look blankly into the distance. Eventually the person will get fed-up of the vacant look on your face and say something like: *'Didn't you hear what I said?'* Slowly turn your eyes in their direction and say in the dullest voice possible: *'Are you trying to tell me something? Unfortunately I don't have any brains so I can't make any sense out of your words!'*

## HAVE YOU MADE YOUR BED?

**O**h dear! You can't win with this one. A quick peep round the door of your room will give you away. But if you've really forgotten how to make a bed, you could try one of these:

**Literal:** No, there wasn't enough wood and I ran out of nails.

**Scientific:** *No, but I have a good reason. I'm partway through an important science project on tissue degeneration and in order to complete this I have to collect samples of dead skin for the next five years. As skin is shed overnight and while we walk about, I can't possibly make my bed or clean my room* (two for the price of one here!) *until I have accumulated a large enough sample.*

**Paranormal:** Yes. I always make my bed, but I don't know how to tell you this – for a long time now strange things have been happening in my room and each time I make my bed a freak whirlwind homes in on it and whips the covers into a heap. Possibly our house is over a leyline or on the site of an ancient temple and this is the cause of the psychic disturbances in my room.

# CLOTHES

(As in: 'Why are your clothes torn?')

Despite the fact that torn clothes are usually more comfortable and add a little style, not everyone is thrilled at the sight of a new rip. If some eagle-eyed adult zaps you with the above question the minute you get in the door, zap 'em right

back with one of these excellent excuses. (However, this may not be the wisest move, so always have an apology in reserve.)

**Righteous:** These are not *my* clothes. On my way home from school I met a very poor person who happened to be wearing identical clothes, except that his/hers were torn. Out of pity for him/her I swapped clothes.

**UFO:** While I was out a spacecraft landed beside me, and a black robot with red eyes came over to where I stood, transfixed by an alien ray. With his metal claws, he grabbed my clothes and said they were the best he'd ever seen: he would have to take samples back to his home planet. There was nothing I could do to stop him!

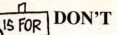

# DON'T

A favourite word of adults, as in: **D**on't touch, **D**on't be cheeky, **D**on't bolt your food, **D**on't answer back, **D**on't be late... Anything you can think of that you want to do, someone will say: *'Don't do that!'* Such a monstrous interruption to the flow of your life often makes you feel like giving a few monstrous reactions. Here are some you can try out:

**Dramatic:** Fall to your knees, clutching your ears and screaming *'Oh! The pain! There's something in my ears! I can't hear a word you say! Help! Help! It's eating my brain away! Are you speaking? I can't hear!'* If you could manage to foam a little at the mouth this would add to the effect.

**Scientific:** Oh no, I wasn't going to. This is a psychological experiment. My teacher asked me to pretend to do something you wouldn't want me to do, and observe your reactions. Any other thoughts you have on the subject are also valuable.

**Wordy:** Here are some monstrously made-up words for an emergency: **bogeyurglebum; collywobbleribbergibber; lollipalurpaloop**.

But **D** is also for **DO**! If you're fed up of **don'ts** and you are feeling a little bit monsterish, try some **DO**s: **DO** wipe your nose on the back of your hand. The snottier, the better. This is especially effective if you can gather a wet, snotty mass and wipe this casually on your sleeve or down your trouser leg. **DO** sneeze wetly and explosively, if possible down the back of the neck of the person in front of you. This is great to do at the cinema. If no one is near, then aim for a good sneeze that can cover a wall or a plate of food!

# EMERGENCY EXCUSE

It's always a good idea to have a few emergency excuses handy for those tricky situations. Here are a few for you to memorise!

Scream – *Eeeeeek!* At the same time rise to your feet, clutch your throat, blink several times, stagger around a bit and then fall to the floor, moaning.

Or you could stun listeners with: *'I'm trying to decide whether or not I concur with your postulate. The basic supposition requires further in-depth thought and cogitation.'*

This one always works a treat: *'Oh, sorry Miss, I was looking for my pet tarantula, it's escaped.'* (This should not only get you out of answering the question, but out of the whole lesson!)

Clap one hand over one eye, produce a glass eye from your pocket and gasp *'Oh! Oh! My eye has fallen out!'*

For this one you'll need to keep a spare kilo of tripe in your pocket. Surreptitiously slip it out, clasp both hands across your stomach with the tripe beneath them, shout: *'Oh No! It's eating its way out of me!'* Slip gracefully to the floor and allow some of the tripe to poke through your fingers.

**E** is also for **Eyes** and **Ears**

All good Little Monsters use their eyes and ears to dramatic effect. Here are a few things you can do with yours.

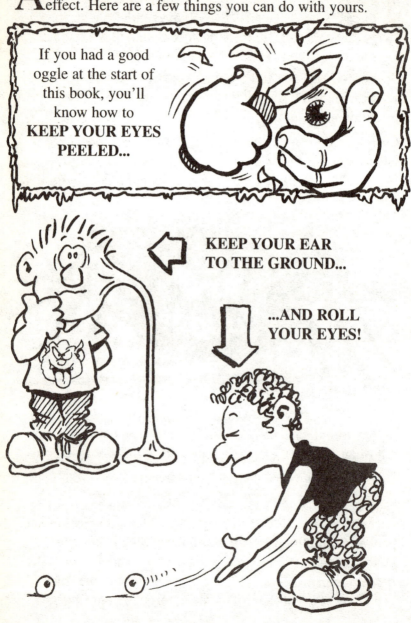

If you had a good oggle at the start of this book, you'll know how to **KEEP YOUR EYES PEELED...**

**KEEP YOUR EAR TO THE GROUND...**

**...AND ROLL YOUR EYES!**

And **E** is for **Expert**...

Teachers always seem to pick on those who DON'T know the answers. They NEVER ask the smug little swots who DO know! Teachers are there to inform, and they can't inform someone who already knows. You can use this fact to your advantage. All little swots read the right books! A teacher has to only take one look at the books that a pupil is carrying to see this kid is already an Expert.

Here's our basic booklist:
*The Origin of the Species*
*The Oxford English Dictionary*
*The Complete Works of Shakespeare*
*An Introduction to Quantum Theory*
*The Economic Implications of Climatic Changes*

Visit the school library regularly. Teachers will come to recognise you as a little Expert and will leave you alone.

E is also for
EXCUSED GAMES!

Do you want to do Cross-country in the pouring rain while your dry, track-suited, teacher drinks coffee in the staff room? NO! Here is a really convincing official note excusing you from PE.

Dear Teacher,

The pupil handing you this letter is part of an international TOP SECRET PROJECT and must under **NO** circumstances engage in PE, Games or Cross-country Running. He/she is an Experimental Biological Hybrid grown in our Laborities at Area 51. He/she must perform NO STRESSFUL OR REPETITIVE EXERCISES! This is a highly sensitive issue and we expect your co-operation in this matter. Please destroy this letter upon reading.

Dr Albert Newton
Director of International Genetic Programming
Megatronics Laboratories

# FARTING

**B**reaking wind in public speaks for itself! No need for elaborate excuses as rooms, even whole buildings, can be cleared within seconds. It is not, of course, considered polite – but if you feel that it is *really* called for, then the truly effective fart must appear natural, surprising even the farter. Try these out for size:

**The Baked Bean Fart:** This fart is short and round but sounds like a rifle shot and startles both the farter and his audience.

**The 'Two For One' Fart:** This is a fart within a fart. First comes a loud, explosive fart then, after a short pause, a second, smaller one. This fart needs careful control, otherwise both farts run into one.

**The Silent But Deadly Fart:** This is a real room-emptier. A 'watch-everyone-run-for-their-gasmasks' fart. Also known as the *Oh Help! Who Did That!* fart. For your own comfort, you may need to keep a peg handy in your pocket.

## FOODS FOR FARTING

The champion farter needs to watch his diet. Only eat those foods which help the farting process. Here are some starters:

BEAKED BEANS  CHICK PEAS
KIDNEY BEANS  ONIONS
SWEETCORN  NUTS  CUCUMBER
EGGS  CURRY  CHILLI  RADISHES

**F** is also for **Frightful Phrases**!

Often parents and teachers will use some monstrous Frightful Phrase. It is well to be prepared for this as you can then ham it up by taking them literally, which will (hopefully!) deflect them from their original gripe!

BUTTON YOUR LIP!

I'VE GOT MY EYE ON YOU!

TAKE THAT SMIRK OFF YOUR FACE!

YOU'LL PAY THROUGH THE NOSE FOR THIS!

I'M STUMPED BY YOUR BEHAVIOUR!

YOU'LL BE LAUGHING ON THE OTHER SIDE OF YOUR FACE!

# GOING

(As in: 'Where are you going?')

Why do they need to know? Because they worry about you! They don't want any harm to come to you. So if you're really going out, tell them **where**. After all, you might get stuck on a barbed wire fence and hang there for hours – just because no one knows where you are! However, if you're actually only going upstairs to read or play a computer game, risk their reaction and sock 'em with one of these:

**Noble:** Actually, I'm just on my way to feed the family of five orphaned vampires that I've been secretly supporting for the past two years. This is no easy task, fitting it around my school work and *all the chores you keep putting on me...*

**Melodramatic:** Throw your hands into the air, clasp one hand to your forehead and give a strangled cry: *'Ohhhhh! What is this? The Spanish Inquisition? All I want is a little freedom, a little peace...'* Sink into a chair, burying your head in your hands at this point.

**Weird:** I'm about to enter the Twilight Zone through a temporal door that opens every third day in the garden shed.

**G** is also for **Get This** and **Get That**!

**D**on't you hate it when you've just settled nicely in front of the TV to watch your favourite soap when some adult calls out: 'Get my glasses!' or 'Go and get your homework!'...

CAN YOU GET ME THE RADIO SO I CAN LISTEN TO IT WHILST I MAKE YOUR TEA, IRON YOUR PE KIT AND DO YOUR LUNCHBOX?

If you want to be left in peace to watch more mind-numbing TV, what you need are a few Monstrously diabolical excuses.

**a)** *Sorry, I can't get up at the moment. Dad/Mum/whoever superglued me to the armchair so that I would be sure to check the next few programs for a TV competition they're doing to win a million pounds!*

**b)** I'd like to do it but I'm doing a school psychology project on human behaviour, and my task is to practice self-assertiveness by consistently refusing to do what I'm asked! You'll have to write down how many times I've overcome my natural desire to help because the more I don't do what I'm asked, the more marks I get!

**c)** *I can't move at the moment 'cos a huge spider has just crossed the room – I think it was a tarantula. You'd better not come in until I'm sure it's safe!*

**IS FOR HOMEWORK**

## HOMEWORK

Somewhere in life you'll meet this one! Some people behave as if the biggest crime on the planet is NOT DOING YOUR HOMEWORK! Not done yours? The **best** excuse, in this situation, is an excuse you won't need to use: doing homework may seem a pain but it's given to help you – so don't grow up to be a Dork! BE SMART! DO YOUR HOMEWORK!

SMARTY FARTY! OH, YUK, HOW BORING! GET REAL–THERE'S NO WAY YOU CAN FIT HOMEWORK AROUND YOUR TV SCHEDULE!

SO GET YER BRAIN CELLS AROUND THESE GREAT EXCUSES!

**Teacher's pet:** This one works best if you've done your homework regularly for a few weeks and made sure you're the first to arrive and the last to leave. If you've also put in some extra groundwork – bringing your teacher wonderful, expensive gifts; hanging around him/her offering to carry books; licking shoes, etc, so much the better. Arrange your face into a distressed expression and say: *'I was in such a rush to get to school – because I love it – that I dropped my book as I was running across the road and a lorry ran over it, totally destroying it and my six hours hard work.'*

**Paranormal:** You'll need a few props for this one, such as a trail of green slime down your jacket. Torn clothes would certainly help the effect – if you need an excuse for these when you get home, just turn to page 15! Open your eyes wide to give yourself a haunted look, and gasp *'Sir! Sir! (or Miss! Miss!) An alien stole my maths book! A huge silver spaceship landed in the school yard as I was coming in the gate. A tall, silver-suited thing grabbed me. I struggled* (here point to your torn clothes) *and managed to get away, but it kept hold of my book and took off with it.'*

**Self-sacrificing:** I was in the bank when a gunman came in and demanded something valuable from everyone. I tried to force my pocket-money on him but he insisted that I show him everything I had on me, and as soon as he saw my beautifully-done homework he took that.

**Protective:** Stand back! It's invisible, there's no rash and the doctor said no one will be able to see how much I'm suffering – BUT NO ONE MUST TOUCH ME OR ANYTHING THAT I HAVE TOUCHED. I'm afraid that means I will have to leave my homework book at home until the doctor says I may touch it again.

 **IS FOR INSULTS**

The well-placed insult can do wonders to get people thinking about things other than the subject in question! The best insults are just dropped casually into the conversation and will have the same effect as telling someone a very large hairy spider is crawling up their leg – ie, they will instantly forget everything else. Before engaging in insult tactics, however, it is advisable to put on a good pair of running shoes...

## TOP TEN MONSTROUS INSULTS!

❶ You've got a face like a million dollars – it's all green and wrinkly.

❷ I never forget a face, but in your case I'll make an exception.

❸ The last time I saw a face like yours, I threw it a fish.

❹ Does your nose pick up all the channels?

❺ He's got two brains cells, one is lost and the other is out looking for it.

❻ I bet your head whistles in a cross wind.

❼ If brains were bird droppings you'd have a clean cage.

❽ I wouldn't say he was filthy but his clothes get dirtier on the inside than the outside.

❾ He's 5 minutes behind everyone else and built to stay that way.

❿ The noise in your head is bothering me.

PLEASE HOLD YOUR BREATH, I'M NOT WEARING A PROTECTIVE SUIT!

 **JELLY**

How did jelly get on there? Why ask you? Everyone knows you only have to take your eyes off jelly for a second and it leaps all over the place. A short answer might be best. The safest one is: 'I don't know' followed by an offer to clean it up. If you must tempt fate though, choose from:

THAT'S NOT JELLY, THAT'S PART OF MY MUCOUS COLLECTION. I'VE BEEN LOOKING FOR IT EVERYWHERE.

I CAN'T UNDERSTAND IT –
IT FELL STRAIGHT THROUGH MY FINGERS!

OH NO! IT'S TRYING TO ESCAPE AGAIN! I TOLD IT TO STAY IN ITS BOX, AND THEY'D BE BACK TO TAKE IT HOME NEXT TIME THEY VISIT THIS PLANET!

It may also be worth pointing out that 'jelly flicking' is part of a long history of childhood tradition! Your parents should be proud that you are keeping this quaint old custom alive.

## K IS FOR KISS

(As in: 'Come and kiss your auntie goodbye.')

I don't know why, but relatives, especially aunties, always want to kiss you. It's not kind to hurt people's feelings but... no self-respecting monster would stand for it! He'd come up with an excuse like this:

> ...YES, WHEN I'VE FINISHED EATING THIS **SPIDER**!

This excuse has even more effect if you can have a half-eaten spider hanging from your mouth – or even a couple of legs sticking out of the side of your mouth helps. It is also good for getting rid of any likely kissers very fast indeed!

Or you could try this: walk towards the boring old sourpuss and assume a sweet smile, then, just as your face is an inch from hers, give a huge, loud belch. That should send her staggering backwards and, with luck, horrify the lot of them. Of course, you may pay for it later so it's best to practice looking surprised and say: 'Oh, excuse me!' As if you have no idea how it happened. **Monsters must be devious.**

### REMEMBER!

### BE PREPARED

NO SELF-RESPECTING MONSTER WOULD EVER VENTURE OUT WITHOUT CHECKING HIS/HER BREATH — THE FOULER THE BETTER! NO ONE WILL WANT TO KISS YOU IF YOUR BREATH STINKS. EXPERIMENT WITH BREATH-STINKING CONCOCTIONS AND KEEP SOME ON YOU. KEEP HALF A RAW ONION IN YOUR POCKET AND IN AN EMERGENCY TAKE A QUICK BITE OF THAT.

ALWAYS EAT LOTS OF GARLIC CHEESE!

## LATE
(As in: 'Why are you late?')

This is a firm favourite of all adults and usually no answer you give will be acceptable, especially if people have been worrying about you! Remember, if you know you're going to be late, the smart thing to do is phone and let someone know that you are safe! Only a real Dork would cause people needless worry! But – if you think everyone is over-reacting, you *could* try to defuse the situation with a monsterish reply, such as:

**Didn't you hear that the Earth's rotational speed has just increased by 30 %? Unfortunately, I'm the only one on Earth not affected by this, and I just couldn't keep up with the space/time continuum. *I'm* not late at all, *you're* all early!**

OK, WHY ARE YOU LATE?

I MET A HEAD BY THE SIDE OF THE ROAD AND IT ASKED ME TO SHOW IT THE WAY TO THE BODYSHOP!

**L** is also for **Listening**, as in: 'Why aren't you listening?'

Sometimes this question seems so unfair. After all, you never ask adults why they are talking in the middle of your daydream! If you are fed-up with people asking you this silly question you could try something like this:

*Scientific:* **I am listening! The subconscious mind hears and stores everything that is said! Nothing is lost. What is the point of wasting the attention of the conscious mind on something that the subconscious does automatically?**

Weird: *What? Oh, Quick! There's something crawling out of my ear!* (Leap up here and stomp on the floor.) *Got it! At last I'm free from the clutches of the alien mind-worm from Alpha Centauri!* Peeling off the previously planted glob of green bubblegum from the sole of your shoe will add a touch of authenticity, as will your total ignorance of anything that was told you during the last month.

## MUD!

(As in: 'Where did that mud come from?')

Any sane monster knows the value of mud. Mud is fun. Mud is necessary. Mud is part of Life! Adults, however, seem to have lost this affinity to mud and can spot a speck of it miles away. One glance and questions come: 'Is that mud on your clothes? Who's been trailing mud across this floor?' At times like these, no excuse will be accepted. The best course is to creep away, taking care not to leave muddy footprints any further than necessary. However, if you're feeling particularly monstrous, try:

**1) I stepped in a puddle and it jumped up and attacked me.**

2) I think the dog's been eating something he shouldn't. Just as I came in the door he was sick all over the floor and this strange brown bile came pouring from him.

**3) Careful – you'll hurt its feelings! This is my new pet, a Mudgalip from Ursa Major. It's on my clothes because you've frightened it, and it's clinging to me for comfort.**

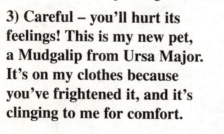

Following on closely is **Mess**, as in: 'Who made this mess?'

Whatever kind of mess it happens to be, people always seem to ask you, as though you are bound to know the answer because you just happen to be in the vicinity! Adults are apt to make these kind of deductions, mainly because they watch too many detective series on TV! Whining and pleading your innocence won't cut any ice – try one of the following:

**New Age: At the moment I don't know who made this mess, but if you'd really like to find out I could try reading the entrails of the chicken in the fridge, or I could dowse for psychic vibrations with my yo-yo! If you start tidying it up I'll go and lie down and try to contact my astral plane to get an answer to your question.**

<u>Intellectual:</u> You have scored five points on my behavioural response chart! This isn't really a mess at all, it's part of my school social studies project! By carefully creating various incidents I can then match your predicted responses to your actual responses. You have been of great help to this project!

**Heroic: Yes, it is a mess, but I couldn't help it. I could only think of catching it before it got out of the room. What? Didn't you see it? It was a huge tarantula! It ran out from under the chair where it was hiding. See, here it is!** *(Hold up tub with large rubber spider inside and rattle for effect.)*

JUST BE CAREFUL TO AVOID THE PSYCHIC SHOCK OF ACTUALLY TIDYING IT UP YOURSELF!

# NOISE

(As in: 'Why are you making that noise?')

What a stupid question. Can you believe it? How can you have a good time without making a noise? How can you do anything without making a noise? Unfortunately grown-ups like peace and quiet and sometimes it's best to humour them and resist giving a Noisy Monster excuse...

**Kind: I'm giving granny a mind-blowing experience. Her life is so boring and dull I thought I'd cheer her up. I've linked her hearing aid to this 140 decibel ghetto blaster that's playing old songs, so she gets a blast from the past...**

**Suffering:** How can I puke quietly? I've been doing my best not to let you see I'm a very sick person, but I can hide it no longer! My stomach is heaving, my guts are churning, and I can't help groaning – and *that's* when you pick on me!

**Scientific:** I'm perfecting my burp and fart synchronisation. I have to keep my bum and stomach muscles under control until the burp has risen into my throat. Then I gently ease the fart down and let it out as the burp shoots into my mouth. I'm probably the only person in the world to have perfected this technique – but *you* have to complain about the noise!

If stumped by a particularly tricky question try the silent *see-how-these-constant-questions-are-affecting-my-nerves* approach. Start furiously biting your nails and spraying the pieces all over the questioner.

# N is also for **Nose!**

A monster's nose is one of the most important parts of his or her anatomy. No nose can be too big. The bigger the nose, the better for smelling with, storing bogeys in or just poking into other folk's business. Here are a few hooters to give you some breathing space...

YOU'LL HAVE TO EXCUSE ME, MY NOSE IS RUNNING AND I HAVE TO CATCH IT!

HAVE YOU HEARD MY NOSE RING?

HE HAD A NOSE FOR THE BIRDS...

NASA ASKED ME TO TRY OUT THIS NEW NOSE CONE!

# **O** IS FOR ODIOUS TRUMPERS!

In monster terms an Odious Trumper is a really neat descriptive remark or put-down geared to make people stop and think! They can be helpful in oral tests – you may find your teachers are so amazed with your replies that they won't ask you any more awkward questions! Also, if you get stuck for descriptive phrases in creative writing you could do worse than drop in an Odious Trumper!

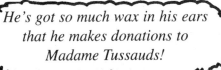

*He's got so much wax in his ears that he makes donations to Madame Tussauds!*

HE HAS A MIND LIKE A STEEL TRAP – FULL OF MICE!

That's an interesting point you made – and I enjoyed the Garlic after-burn too!

My mum says it's good to share things – so would you like some head lice?

*Your brilliance would terrify a lettuce!*

*Would you like to see a free demonstration of Projectile Vomiting?*

IF ONLY HE'D BEEN MORE HANDSOME HE COULD HAVE BEEN A GARGOYLE!

O is also for **Other O**s...

Why do you always leave the door open? Where's your other shoe? Don't open that! If only you'd listen... **What you need for the objectionable Os is an Odious Ogre. Your own pet ogre – he simply eats awkward questioners! However, before you rush out to buy one, study the chart below to decide what type you need.**

**Grade 1 Ogre:** A usually placid Ogre whose temper is only roused by prattish questions like *'Are you going out?'* as you step out the front door.

**Grade 2 Ogre:** Not as easy-going as a Grade 1 Ogre, but still fairly pleasant – and with a really effective temper when a questioner comes on the scene! You'll find your life more peaceful as folks learn to confine their remarks to: *'Yes' 'No'* or *'Anything you say.'*

**Grade 3 Ogre:** Needs plenty of respect. He'll repay you by forgiving you the odd remark that sounds too much like a question, while ensuring your *own* life is free from endless questions and nagging.

**Grade 4 Ogre:** Needs to be treated with extreme caution, even by its owner. Anything that sounds like a question will rouse him to eat anyone in sight. For a life free from the constant stress of finding answers and excuses, this is the Ogre for you!

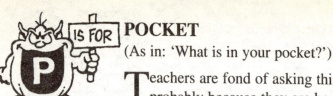

# POCKET

(As in: 'What is in your pocket?')

Teachers are fond of asking this – probably because they are bored, and imagine the contents of your pocket to be more interesting than the piece of chalk in their own. Try some of these monstrous replies...

 MY BAG OF BOGEYS.

*My pet tarantula. I had to bring it with me today – its eggs are hatching.*

My pet snake – I brought it with me today because its skin is shedding and I didn't want it to feel cold.

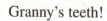 A PIECE OF FLUFF, SOME JELLY, A MOULDY SANDWICH, A DRIED FROG, AND A DRIED BOGEY.

Granny's teeth!

 *A dead rat!*

## Another great **P** is for **Putrid Pets**

If words fail you in a sticky situation, then a quick flash of your putrid pet can drive all thoughts of the subject in question out of the mind of your accuser and have him/her running for cover. Here are few you can try out:

**Pet Leech:** Cut the stalk from a mushroom and put the top in a plastic bag with a big dollop of tomato sauce. Shake it up! When it's time, take the bag out of your pocket and yell: *'Aaaarh! My pet leech has burst its blood sac!'*

**Pet Maggots:** Cut a kiwi fruit into the rough shape of a mouse, add a piece of boiled spaghetti for the tail, and place it in a plastic tub. Carefully stick on bits of shed cat fur or fluff. Arrange some rice pudding on the 'mouse', making sure the mouse shape and fluff are still visible. In a desperate situation, take off the lid and say: *'Oh look! My pet maggots are hatching out of the dead mouse!'*

**Pet Tapeworm:** Get the longest piece of flat ribbon pasta that you can find. Place it in a bowl of water and leave it until it is soft. Pour away the water. Brush the pasta with salad cream and red food colouring and put into a plastic bag. At the appropriate moment wave the bag around and yell: *'Oh yuk! My pet tapeworm is regurgitating its food!'*

# QUIBBLE

If you want to be a Little Horror in class or a Little Monster at home, you must become an Experienced Quibbler. Never answer a question straight away or obey an instruction if you can quibble about it. Here are a few monsterish quibbles.

I can't eat that, the alien host inside me would die.

I CAN'T EAT THAT, IT'S NOT BLUE.

*What proof have you for that statement? Have you been to the outer reaches of the galaxy?*

How many times has it made you sick?

*But what if this is not reality? How do I know you're not a figment of my imagination?*

Can millions of lemmings be wrong? What do they know that we don't?

## Q is also for **Quick Quotes**

Adults like quotations. It gives them the feeling you've been studying hard. Tuck these useful quotes away for special occasions when a quick quote will quell a question. Spread your arms wide and quote:

*Hey, Diddle, Diddle,*
*The cat and the fiddle,*
*The cow jumped over the moon*
*and a large cow pat is now orbiting the planet.*

To be or not to be that is the gurgensplatzer.

*It's never too late to fart.*

Twinkle, twinkle little spotty,
I think you look a little dotty!

Or, if your quotes don't work, you could try...

...A QUICK **QUASIMODO** IMPRESSION!

# ROTTEN REPORT

This is a tough one to get out of because it's down in black and white, or on a computer somewhere. The best thing to do is have a quick look *before* handing it to your parents and then don't give it to them until *after* you have made it sound *much* worse than it is! That way, even if it is bad, they'll think it's not *as* bad as your version of it! However, if your report really is that rotten, you could try one of the following ploys:

**1) Build a disintegrator. Vaporise your report then disintegrate the school computer, the filing cabinet and any piles of paper in the office. Just to be sure, disintegrate your entire classroom!**

2) Wrap a lump of raw steak around your report and throw it into a garden where you know a Rottweiler lives!

**3) Send your report in a plain, brown envelope to NASA, asking them to put it on the next probe heading out of the Solar System!**

4) Tell your teacher your parents have gone away to Peru to look for a lost civilisation. Ask him/her to send your report by air mail to: 13, Yucatan Place, Guatemala, Peru.

## R is also for **Useful Remarks**

**K**eep a stock of useful remarks. These are not necessarily excuses or answers to the questions asked, but thrown suddenly into a conversation can confuse things quite nicely.

**Did you know there's a big green thing with ten legs hanging from your nose?**
I don't know what has happened to the dog but his eyes have turned red and he's covered in green slime. Oh, if you're going to look for him, he's in the kitchen cooking lunch.
**I wouldn't do that if I were you, the last person to touch that is now part of my mucus collection.**
Help! Help! Protect me! The voices have started again! This time they're coming for me. We must have silence! If we're all very quiet maybe they won't track me down.

AAARGH! QUICK! RUN! MY PET TAPEWORM HAS JUST ESCAPED AND IS LOOKING FOR A NEW HOST!

# SCHOOL

Teachers have many unpleasant habits, not least sneaking up on you with awkward questions when you least expect them. BE PREPARED. The safest course is to pay attention so you can shock them by knowing the right answer. Failing that, surprise them with a **snap-back**:

**I wish you'd pay a little attention**
    – I'm paying as little as I can!
**You should have been here at 9 o'clock**
    – Why? What happened?
**You can't sleep in class**
    – I could if you didn't talk so loudly!
**Why are you late?**
– An alien called to borrow my dictionary!

Then there are the sneaky questions aimed to seek out the gaps in your knowledge. But we can all be sneaky, can't we?

**What's a gross?**
– 144 monsters all dribbling
    and drooling pus.
**Where are the Andes?**
– At the end of the armies.
**Who was Hamlet?**
    – Piglet's son.
**Who said 'Eureka'?**
– I don't know, but you don't
    smell too good yourself!

## S is also for **Shopping**

Can you go shopping for me? Don't you just love that one? Adults have lots of chores to get through *and* you to feed, so it wouldn't hurt you, would it? Still, if you're feeling monsterish, try:

**Weird:** Throw your head back, grasp your throat with both hands and stagger round the room gasping and gurgling.

**Sorrowful:** I'd love to go shopping but unfortunately I can't move. While I was out I walked in some purple goo and I've noticed that not only are my feet now stuck to the floor but a numbness has been creeping up my body. It has reached my hips. Soon I may not even be able to ta...

**Willing but simple:** *Yes, of course I'll go. Now, what was that again: a jottle of bam, a sliced head, a mub of targ...*

**Sick Note:** Trace over the sick note below and just fill in the blanks, cross out 'he' or 'she', and sign it in your best doctor's signature. This need only be a scribbly scrawl as no-one can ever read doctors' handwriting anyway.

# DOCTOR'S
# MEDICAL CERTIFICATE

Date...........................

Dear ..........................................

.................................... was unable to attend your class yesterday because he/she had a bug. It is a particularly nasty little bug, biting and pinching and making a general nuisance of itself until the child agrees not to go to school that day. Unfortunately, there is nothing that can be done about it.

Doctor .......................................

# When all else fails – SCREEEAAM!

A blood-curdling scream will stop even the most determined interrogator dead in their tracks. Get as close as you can, and

## YELL!

AAAAARGH!

If there is one thing monsters are good at it's being scary! Some strange people even think monsters *look* scary! Although I'm sure *you* can't imagine how anyone could be scared of a harmless, three-eyed, hairy green monster, or a sweet little, one-eyed blue ogre. Scary is fun. Scary is **very effective**! Here are some monster expressions to try out:

# TIME

(As in: 'What time do you call this?')

Tempting to think up some good names, isn't it? If, however, you are feeling meek, bite your tongue and answer, *'Half-past ten. Am I late? I'm sorry'*. If you really don't care what happens to you, though, what the heck – try something like:

**a) Fred Spizenburger.**

**b) Time to catch that giant beetle crawling up your leg.**

**c) Time to step back, I'm about to throw up.**

**d) Time to assume my normal shape – I'm really an alien from the planet Zarg.**

Or, if you want to throw the questioner completely off the scent, scream: *'YIIIKKKKKES! What's that hanging from your nose/crawling up your skirt/sitting on your hair?'*

**T** is also for **Tidy**, as in: 'Why can't you tidy your room?'

Your idea of tidy and your Mum or Dad's idea are *two different things*. Unfortunately for you, if you want a peaceful life you'll have to conform to their view. Don't wait until you are walking on three layers of mugs, old toast, orange peel, coke cans, CDs, and assorted clothes – adults seem to find this annoying. A real monster, of course, will always try to wriggle out of the situation:

**Puzzled:** It *is* tidy! I even picked up my clothes, disturbing the mice nesting in them. I can't see what is untidy about it!

**Reasonable:** I would like to tidy my room but unfortunately I've developed an allergy to dirt, fluff and bedrooms. When I touch *anything* with the intention of tidying it, my hands itch and I come out in a blue and purple rash. I went to the doctor without telling you (I didn't want to worry you), but he says I will have to avoid tidying rooms for the rest of my life.

# USEFUL THINGS

A few monsterish things hidden somewhere nearby help distract questioners from what they were about to ask you:

**Tomato sauce:** Keep a large dollop of this in your pocket. Then in an emergency, stick your hand into your pocket, give a sharp cry and draw it out with the fingers covered in blood!

**Bottled Pong:** A really lethal weapon. Fill an empty bottle with pieces of cheese, raw onion, garlic and anything else you can think of. Put the top back on the bottle and store for several weeks. Open as and when you want to cause a stink!

**Mouldy Cheese:** Nurture a small piece of cheese until it is green and pongy. Wave it under your questioner's nose just as he or she takes a deep breath, preparing to launch into '*Where were you...*' etc.

**Dead Fish:** Another wonderful weapon. Not only does the fish whiff fantastically after a while, but the longer it is in your pocket, the more fluff, snot, gum, sticks to it, doubling its grisly apeararance.

# VILE

VILE is an anagram of EVIL, and it is also what all monsters aim to be. The monster aura – the **Vile Field** – was discovered by Sidney Vile who was the Vilest but has now cleaned up his act and is an **X-Vile**. It was Sidney Vile who drew up the *Vile Effect Chart* (see below).

| VILE EFFECT CHART | |
|---|---|
| **VILE ACTION** | **VILE FIELD EFFECT** |
| WEARING GRANNY'S FALSE TEETH TO FRIGHTEN FOLK AT HALLOWE'EN. | |
| PUKING IN THE PICNIC BASKET. | |
| COLLECTING SPIDERS, SLUGS, SLIME AND SNOT. | |
| BELCHING AND FARTING WHEREVER YOU GO. | |

## V is also for **Vacant Expressions**

A vacant expression is an asset when asked to do some boring chore. Just looking vaguely helpful but incredibly dim comes naturally to a monster. *You* may need to practice:

Hello! Is There Anybody There?

Are We Making Contact?

Is the Brain Connecting?

The Light Is On But Is Anyone Home?

If you'd like a more colourful expression, you could try:

**VOMIT**

**Mix up some fruit yogurt (the lumpy type) with some rice pudding. At a convenient moment fill your mouth, make retching noises, and spew! Mumble –** *'Excuse me I have to leave the room!'* **Sit in the bathroom making loud vomiting noises and apply a bit of green eye shadow to your cheeks, just for extra effect. Then go and watch your favourite TV programme, keeping the noises going.**

# WEIRD

Be Weird! Be Wacky! Cultivate a reputation for being weird and it's not likely that you'll get asked to do chores at home or answer questions in class.

Dress weird!

Act weird!

Talk weird!

YETH! THE ANSWER'S OBLIVIOUS! IT WAS A CRUD MATHS PEST BUT I NEWT ELEVENTYSIX WAS A LONG DERISION! WHAT A GAFF, HE, HE!

## W is also for **Where have you put the... ?**

This question is another favourite. No matter what is missing you get the blame. Sometimes you are to blame! If so – own up! If they're just being unfair as usual, try these:

**Sinister:** I think for your own good it's best you don't know. Please don't force me on this one. I took an oath to protect you, *so don't ask any more!* If you force me to tell you, you'll regret it for the rest of your life which, unfortunately, will not be very long if you meddle any further in this matter.

*Vague: This is where the vacant looks you've practised come in. Assume a pleasant but stupid grin, put your hand to your mouth and say er and um a lot. 'Let me er see um did I er put it in the um bread bin er or was it um...' If you ramble on for long enough the person asking will get fed-up and look for the thing themselves. As it will be someone else who lost it, <u>not you</u>, this seems a reasonable move.*

**Paranormal:** The oddest thing happened. Just as I picked it up a blue light filled the room and a disembodied voice said, *'Put that down. What you hold is the key to mankind's future. It cannot be left in your hands. Stand back and watch.'* Needless to say, I stood back, and a large hand came out of nowhere and picked it up. Then both it and the blue light vanished...

# X-RATED EXERCISES

If you want to be consistently excused for the stupid things you've done, you need to be seen doing this routine of specially formulated exercises. People will realise you're not responsible for your actions *and they'll stop pestering you*!

**Sit-ups:** These need to be done daily in a large bath of cold custard.

**Sty-Chi:** Do this in a pig sty with the pigs. Move slowly on all fours, pausing now and then to lick muck off the pigs.

**Hand-stands:** For this exercise you need to find a field with plenty of cow-pats in it. Do a hand-stand and walk on your hands, making sure you pass at least once through each cow pat.

# YAWN

More boring questions? Just yawn them away. Open your mouth wide to reveal the frog in the back of your throat: wheeze that it has a cold and is too ill to even croak an answer.

**The really effective yawn** has to be of the earsplitting variety, but a few little delicate *'I'm getting bored now!'* yawns will help to get your message across! Usually, though, adults don't get the hint and you'll have to trust to the mega-mouth yawn...

## Z IS FOR ZINGY ZONES

The zingier you are, the more likely it is that you'll not be asked to tea with auntie and be able to keep unwelcome visitors at bay. If you want to increase your whiff capacity, study the following diagram:

❶ **Fart zone** – peas, beans, onions and fizzy pop.

❷ **Mega-fart zone** – curry, garlic, rhubarb and pickled onions.

❸ **BO zone** – body odour from not washing for weeks.

❹ **O zone** – strong body odour from not washing for months or even years and never changing clothes.

❺ **Bad breath zone** – eating garlic, onions and hot peppers.

❻ **Puke zone** – unwashed sicky clothes from constant puking.

❼ **Putrid pocket zone** – anything left to rot or die in pockets, especially strong if moulds, spores and fungi are involved.

❽ **Phew! Smelly feet zone** – hot, sweaty unwashed feet. Best results from wearing thick woolly socks inside hobnailed boots or wellies and never changing them.

And, finally, **Z** is for **Zimmer Frame**.

If you want to live long enough to push a zimmer frame around, (your own, that, is not your granny's), it may be a good idea to keep this book safe from the prying peepers of the adults in your life – they may be feeling monstrous too!

# THE
# KOP-OUT KIT

### also known as the
### KEEP ONE JUMP AHEAD KIT

A pocket-sized, handy reference kit of answers for any possible question. When caught without a quick quip, revolting response or silly solution, quickly kop-in with a kop-out.

HERE IS A SMALL SELECTION FROM THE MANY ANSWERS YOUR KIT CONTAINS:

* *Nine hundred and eighty four*
* **Only those with four eyes and a squint**
* *Frogspawn hunting on the upper reaches of the Ganges*
* **Purple slime with yellow phlegm**
* *Spit three times, turn around twice and throw your wooden leg over your right shoulder*
* **I don't know, but the walls must be really damp**
* *It's better than a drooling problem fart-face*
* **That's where the dog puked**

# BRAIN EXTENSION KIT

**Problems remembering your name
or your way home?
Don't know your ear from your elbow?
Got the I.Q. of an ice-cube?
One sandwich short of a picnic?**

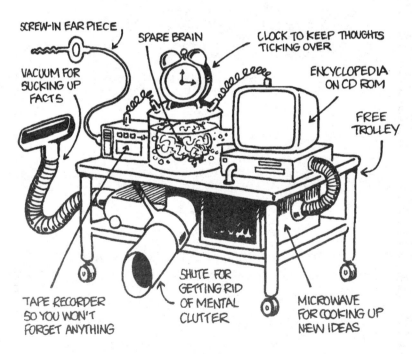

# DON'T DELAY - ORDER TODAY!

# ADULT PHOBIA?

Do you check for grown-ups under the bed? Are you afraid of teachers in the dark? Spooked by shadows and in dread of dark corners? You need ADULT SPRAY. Carry this handy-sized spray around in your pocket and you need never fear adults again. Just one squirt of Adult Spray at the merest sight of an adult, and he or she will be banished for ever.